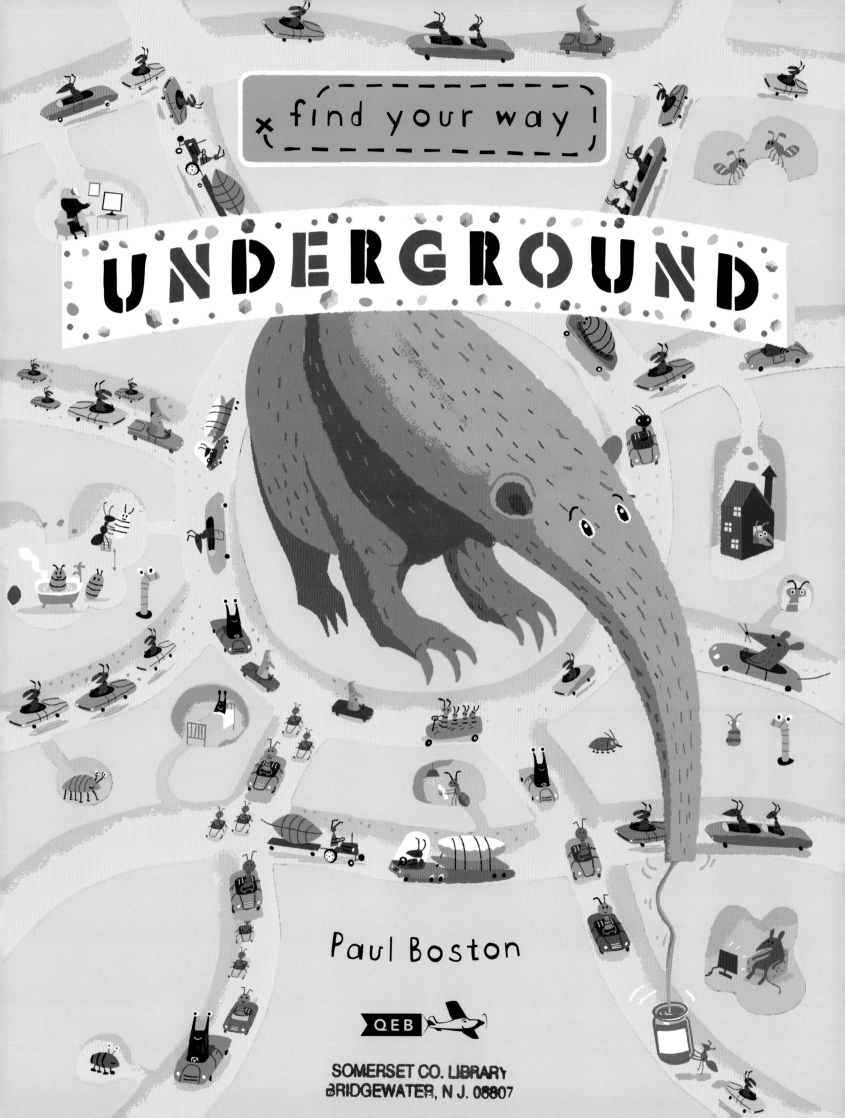

# find your way

# UNDERGROUND

## Paul Boston

QEB

# YOUR MISSION

Us Gnomes are in trouble!
Luna the dragon has stolen our gold.
Are you brave enough to help us get it back?
Find your way to Luna's lair by choosing which
exits or entrances to follow on each page.

## 1
### Choose your transport

Wagon

Frog

Giant Earthworm
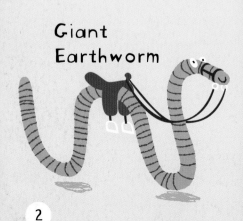

## 2
### Trace a route

There are lots to choose from and you can go **BACKWARD** and **FORWARD** along the same tunnel.

## 3
### Collect on every page

Choose **ONE** of the missions below to help the Gnomes. You will find one of each object in every scene.

Collect 12 **BUCKETS OF WATER** to put out Luna's fires.

Collect 12 **WHEELBARROWS** to pick up all the gold.

Collect **12 MAGIC FLUTES** to play a special tune that will send Luna off to sleep.

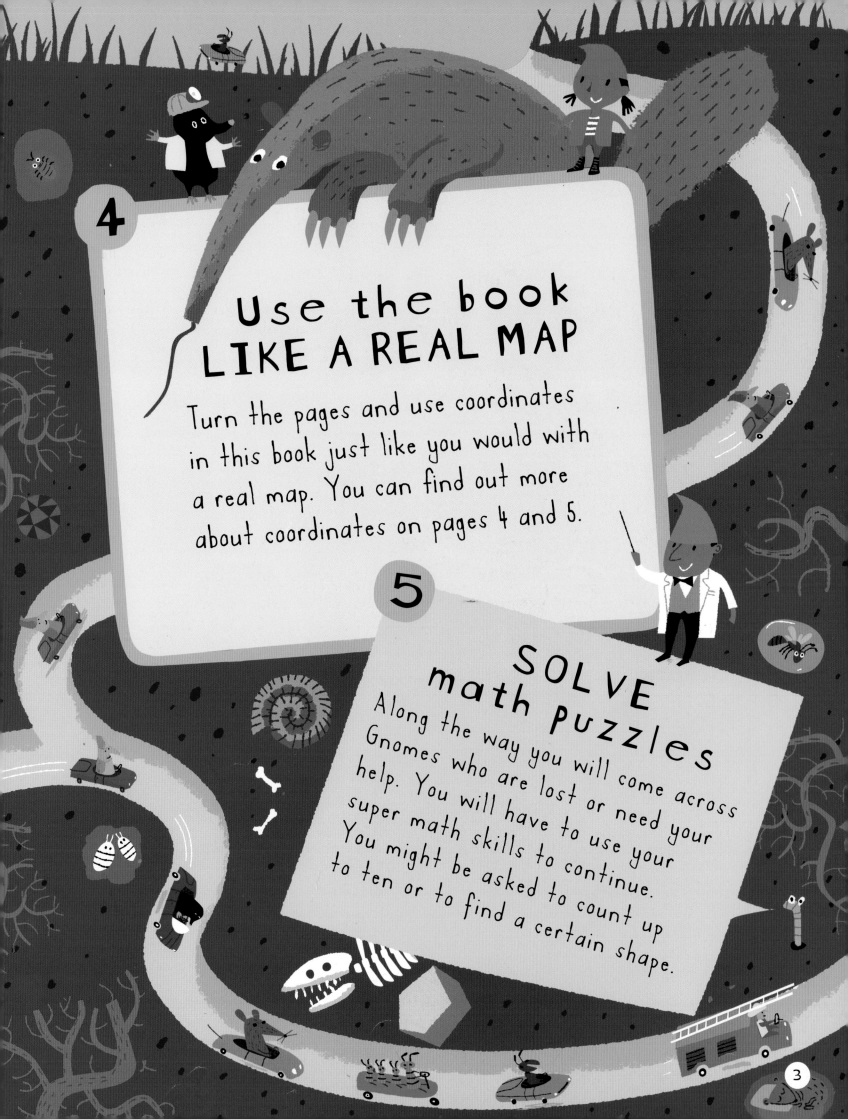

**4**

# Use the book LIKE A REAL MAP

Turn the pages and use coordinates in this book just like you would with a real map. You can find out more about coordinates on pages 4 and 5.

**5**

# SOLVE math puzzles

Along the way you will come across Gnomes who are lost or need your help. You will have to use your super math skills to continue. You might be asked to count up to ten or to find a certain shape.

# Welcome to Gnome City

Look at the map of Gnome City. Can you see where Luna's lair is?
It looks like a castle. That's where you need to get to. Let's use
coordinates to help us describe where Luna's lair is on the map.

START HERE

**A**

Anteater
Junction
Pages 6–7

Vegetable
Plot
Pages 8–9

**B**

**3**

Hidden
Lagoon
Pages 14–15

Egyptian
Tombs
Pages 16–17

**2**

Busy
Beehive
Pages 22–23

Sleepy
Nest
Pages 24–25

**1**

When reading
coordinates:
**crawl ACROSS the
tunnel first, and then
UP the ladder.**

**A**

**B**

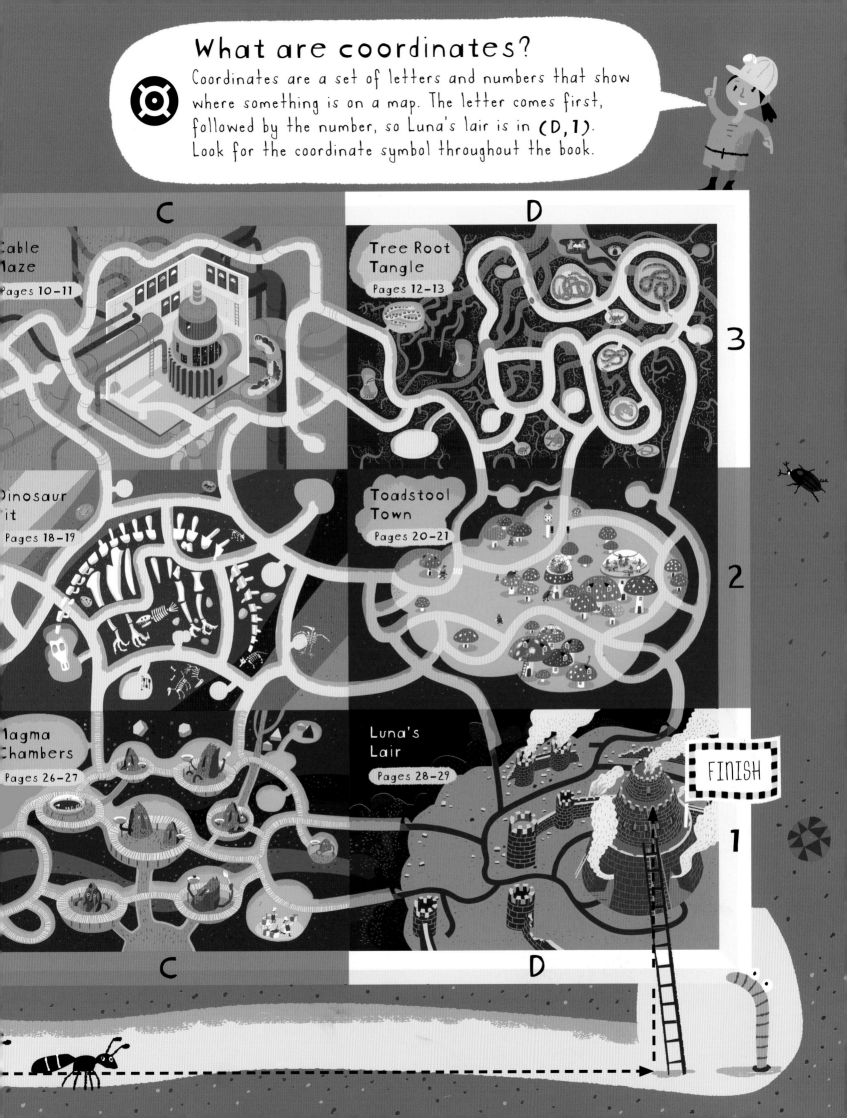

# What are coordinates?

Coordinates are a set of letters and numbers that show where something is on a map. The letter comes first, followed by the number, so Luna's lair is in **(D,1)**. Look for the coordinate symbol throughout the book.

Cable Maze
Pages 10-11

Tree Root Tangle
Pages 12-13

Dinosaur Pit
Pages 18-19

Toadstool Town
Pages 20-21

Magma Chambers
Pages 26-27

Luna's Lair
Pages 28-29

FINISH

C

D

3

2

1

C

D

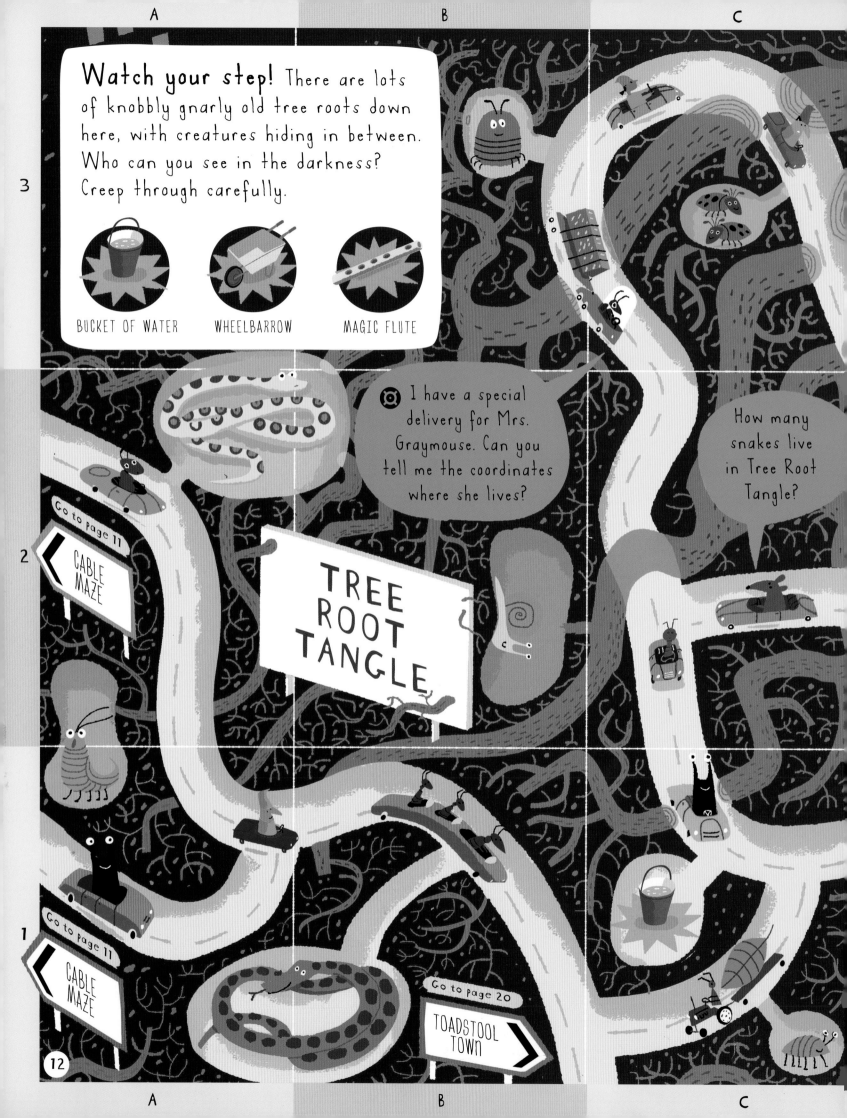

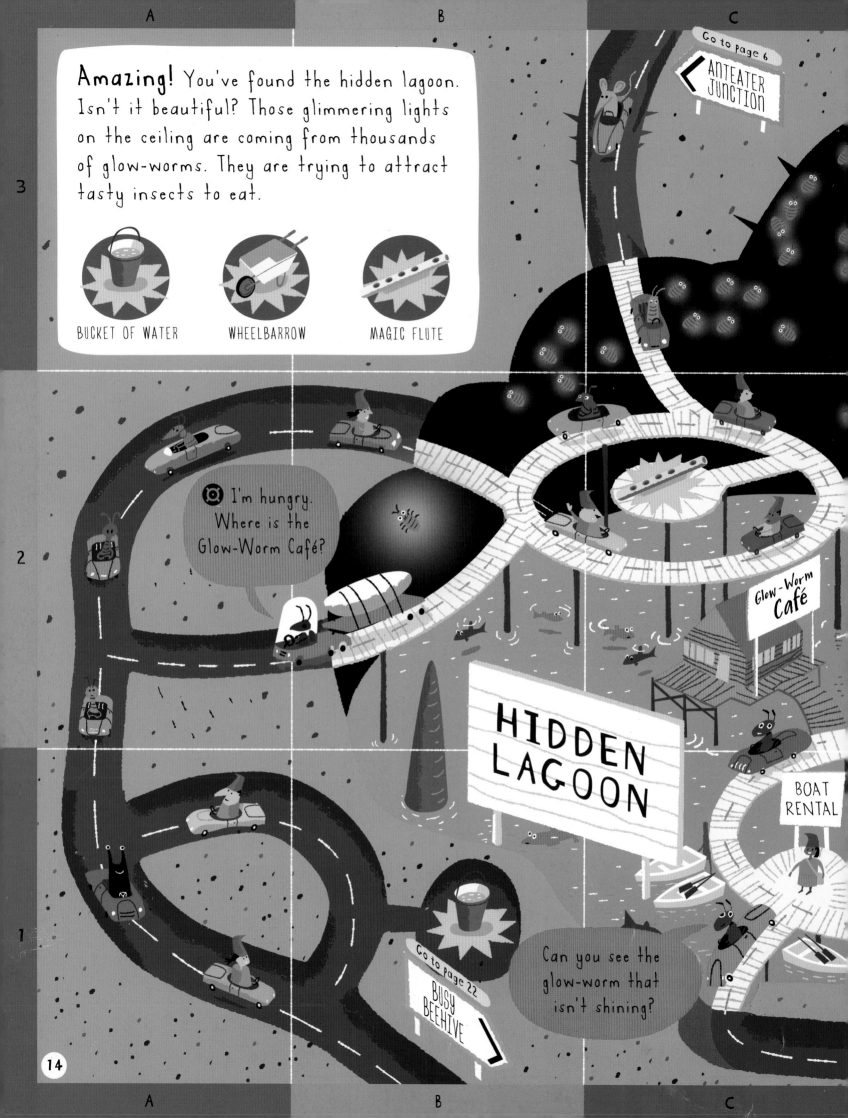

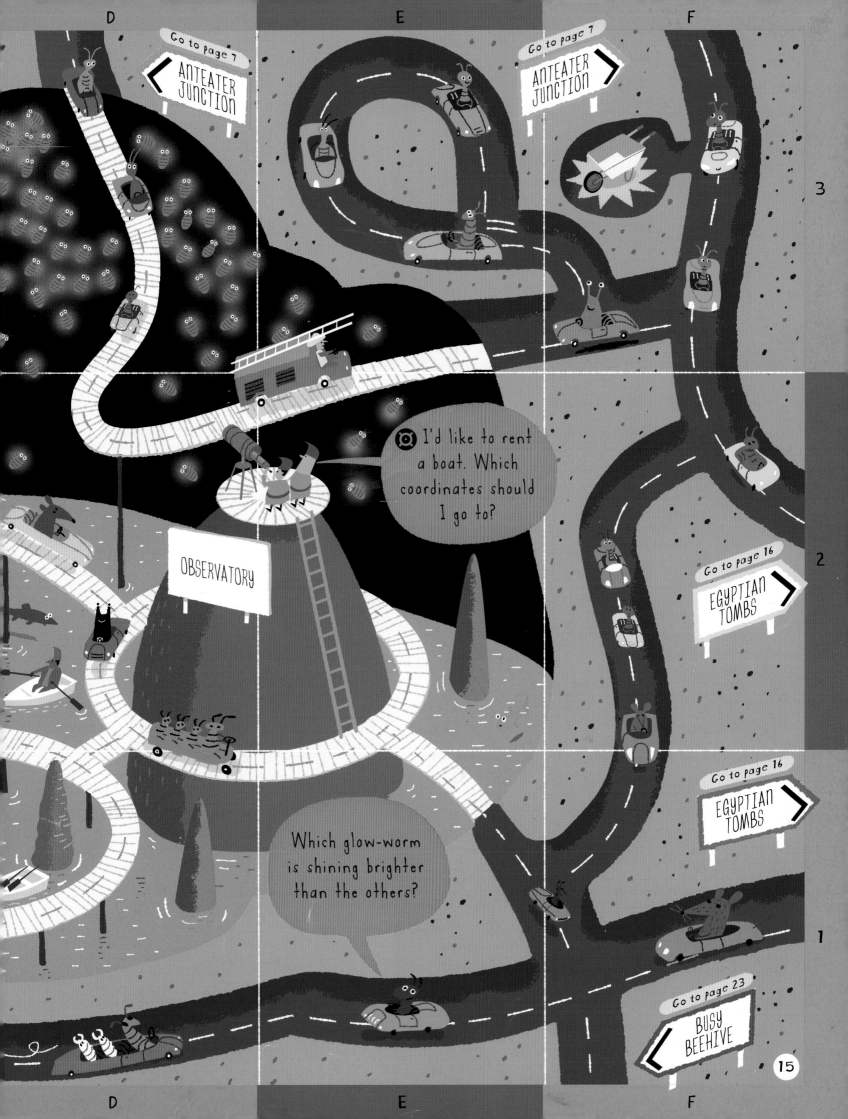

Go to page 9
VEGETABLE PLOT

Go to page 9
VEGETABLE PLOT

Go to page 18
DINOSAUR PIT

Go to page 18
DINOSAUR PIT

Which shapes can you see in the pattern on the walls?

Go to page 25
SLEEPY NEST

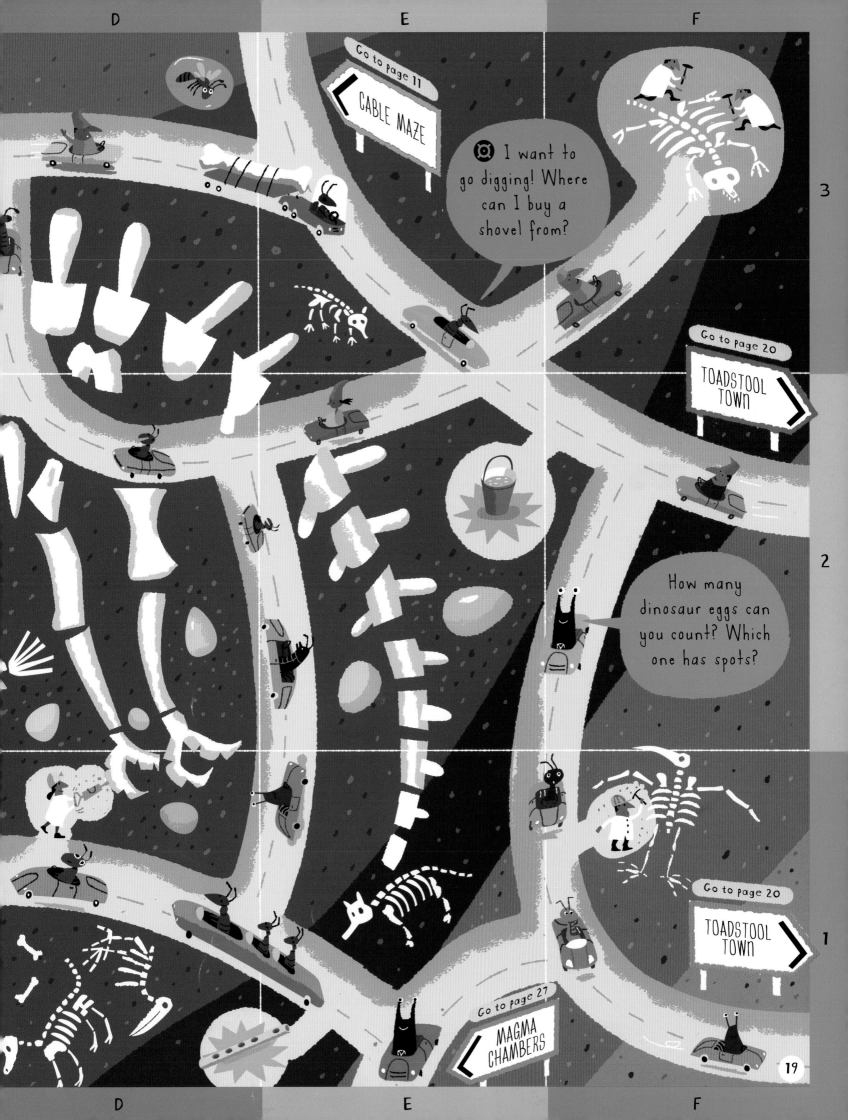

Hooray! You've reached Toadstool Town. The Gnomes have made their homes here from lots of colorful spotted toadstools. What else can you see?

BUCKET OF WATER

WHEELBARROW

MAGIC FLUTE

Go to page 12
TREE ROOT TANGLE

Who lives in the smallest purple toadstool?

Go to page 19
DINOSAUR PIT

TOADSTOOL TOWN

Go to page 19
DINOSAUR PIT

Go to page 28
LUNA'S LAIR

20

Shhh. The armadillos are sleeping! They've curled themselves up into balls and can sleep for 18 hours a day. Tiptoe through their dens to continue on your way. Who else is asleep?

BUCKET OF WATER

WHEELBARROW

MAGIC FLUTE

Go to page 16
EGYPTIAN TOMBS

Go to page 23
BUSY BEEHIVE

Oh no! Which clock has stopped working?

Bedtime drinks

Go to page 23
BUSY BEEHIVE

SLEEPY NEST

Go to page 23

# MORE FUN UNDERGROUND!

## Understanding Coordinates

Encourage your child to look at other places where they might find coordinates, such as on an A-Z map. Draw an underground map together and plan your route to the buried treasure.

## Counting

Go back through the book and look for more opportunities to encourage counting underground. How many legs does a beetle have? How many bees are making honey?

## Telling the Time

Together with your child, draw pictures of their daily routine and cut them out. These could include: waking up, having breakfast, going to school, having dinner, and going to bed. Jumble up the pieces and ask them to put them in the correct order. Use a clock to discuss with your child at which time they carry out each activity. Talk about nocturnal creatures and the differences in their routine.

## Recognizing Shapes

Use cardboard boxes and tubes to encourage underground small world play. Explain the boxes and tubes are similar to burrows and tunnels underground. Use the names of 3D shapes to describe the tunnels and burrows, e.g. cube, cylinder.

## Math Problems and Vocabulary

Look for opportunities to build on mathematics vocabulary and problem solving skills. For example, if there are five Gnomes holding two buckets of water each, how many buckets are there altogether? Try to spot preposition vocabulary such as "above," "below," or "under."

## Measurements

Use a magnifying glass and explore the outdoors. What can you see hiding in the soil? Can you find a long worm? How about a small ant? Guess how many inches you think each one is.

**QuartoKnows**

Quarto is the authority on a wide range of topics.
Quarto educates, entertains and enriches the lives of our readers—enthusiasts and lovers of hands-on living.
www.quartoknows.com

Written and edited by: Joanna McInerney and the QED team
Designed by: Mike Henson
Consultant: Alistair Bryce-Clegg

Copyright © QEB Publishing 2017

First published in the United States by
QEB Publishing, Inc.
6 Orchard
Lake Forest, CA 92630

A catalog record for this book is available from the Library of Congress.

ISBN 978 1 68297 046 1

Printed in China

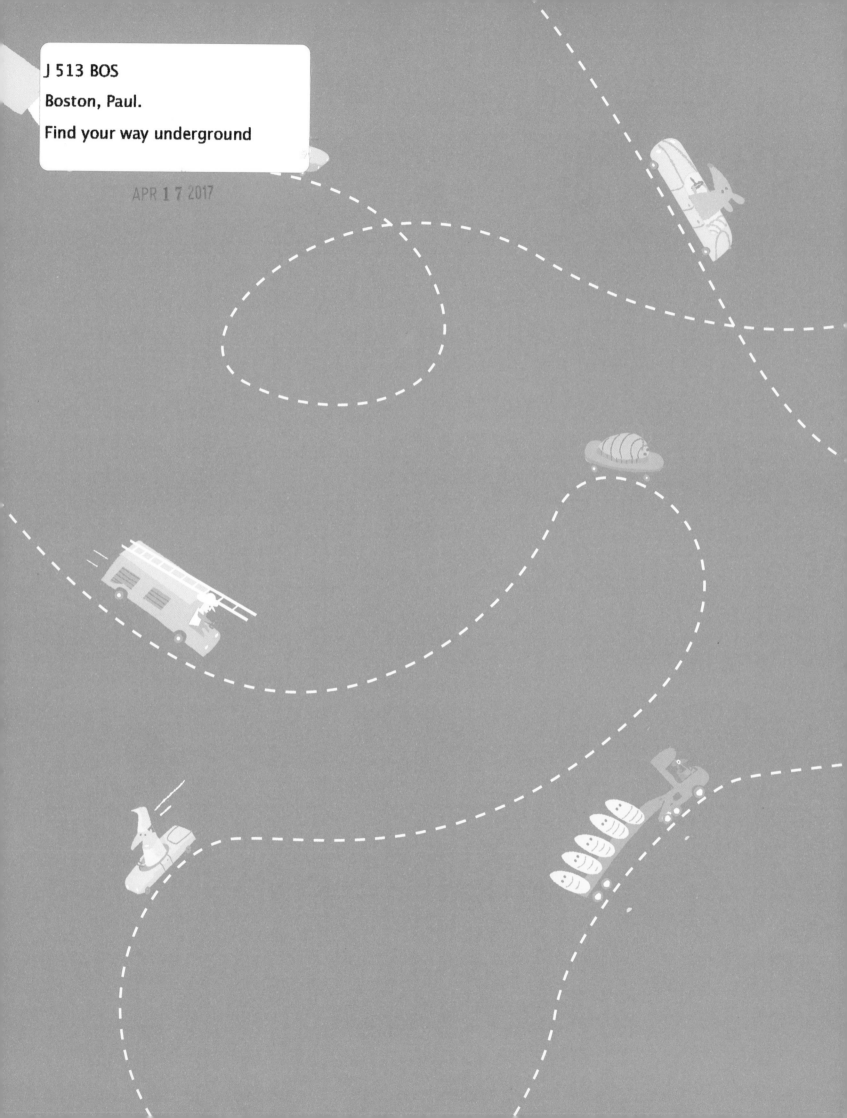